IMAGES
of America

CALIFORNIA STATE
PARK RANGERS

Galen Clark was appointed state guardian of Yosemite on May 21, 1866. Clark was California's and the nation's first park ranger. Yosemite Valley and the Mariposa Grove of Big Trees were California state parks from 1864 until they were returned to federal control in 1906. Clark is pictured here in a photo-card that he apparently handed out while guardian.

ON THE COVER: Ranger James Whitehead assists visitors at the California State Parks exhibit at the 1949 State Fair. Whitehead had a long and distinguished career with California State Parks, rising through the ranks to retire as regional director for Southern California. After retirement, he was appointed and served as a commissioner on the California State Park and Recreation Commission. (Courtesy of California State Parks.)

IMAGES
of America

CALIFORNIA STATE PARK RANGERS

Michael G. Lynch

ARCADIA
PUBLISHING

Published by Arcadia Publishing
Charleston, South Carolina

Printed in the United States of America

Library of Congress Catalog Card Number: 2008933030

For all general information contact Arcadia Publishing at:
Telephone 843-853-2070
Fax 843-853-0044
E-mail sales@arcadiapublishing.com
For customer service and orders:
Toll-Free 1-888-313-2665

Visit us on the Internet at www.arcadiapublishing.com

Author Michael G. Lynch started his career as a California State Park ranger in 1972. Lynch retired in 2003 with 31 years of service. He continues to work half-time as an acting superintendent and supervisor of the environmental resource group at the Auburn State Recreation Area. Lynch is the author of four books and is the acknowledged historian for state park rangers.

CONTENTS

ACKNOWLEDGMENTS

First, I would like to thank Brian Smith, Karen Smith, and Donna Howell for proofreading the draft of this book. I would also like to thank John Cleary, Steve Huntington, Rodi Lee, Patsy Lynch, Scott Liske, Doug Messer, Lynn Rhodes, Brian Robertson, Jacob Rubinstein, and Michael Whitehead for their assistance to me in producing this book. I also appreciate the support given by the California State Park Rangers Association (CSPRA) and the State Park Peace Officers Association of California (SPPOAC) who have done and continue to do a great job of representing rangers in the professional and labor aspects their job.

Unless otherwise noted, all images appear courtesy of the State Park Ranger Anniversary Photograph Collection. As noted in the captions, other images in this volume appear courtesy of California State Parks (CSP) and the Yosemite National Park Research Library (YNPRL).

INTRODUCTION

The public's image of a state park ranger's job is idealistic, romantic, and in large part, positive. A park ranger is the combination of many things. They are explorers, guardians, outdoorsmen (and later outdoors persons), educators, police officers, tree lovers, nature guides, greeters, animal protectors, custodians of our natural wonders, and field environmental scientists all rolled into one. All these aspects form part of the ideal and real park ranger. Add to this the fact that a ranger works mainly in spectacular natural or historically significant areas and you have quite a package. No doubt, this is why rangers are often idolized and considered American icons by the public.

On the more mundane, day-to-day level, however, with ever-increasing numbers of visitors and declining budgets, today's rangers must act more often as law enforcement officers, rescuers, and emergency medical responders. With low staffing levels and relatively low pay, the modern state park ranger is often working without sufficient staff, long hours, and alone. The unfortunate results of these factors are that rangers in many parks are not as readily available to perform the more positive aspects of the job, like interpretation/outdoor education, providing information, resource management, and ensuring that visitor services like campgrounds and day-use areas are running smoothly.

Historically, when Yosemite pioneer Galen Clark was named "Guardian of Yosemite" on May 21, 1866, he became the first person to be formally appointed and paid to protect and administer a great nature park. Clark had become California's and the nation's first park ranger.

Clark's precedent-setting appointment was the result of federal legislation signed into law by Abraham Lincoln on June 30, 1864. This law granted the Yosemite Valley and the Mariposa Grove to the State of California with the "express condition that the premises shall be held for public use, resort and recreation . . . inalienable for all time." Yosemite became the first large natural area, state or national, to be established for such park purposes. It was not until eight years later that Yellowstone was set aside as what would be considered America's first national park.

It took the state legislature nearly two years to officially accept Yosemite and the Mariposa Grove of Big Trees. However, in another unprecedented move, the bill accepting the federal grant provided for an eight-member board of commissioners to manage the Yosemite Valley and Mariposa Grove and gave authority to the commission "to appoint a guardian . . . to perform such duties as they may prescribe, and to receive such compensations they may fix, not to exceed five hundred dollars per annum." At the first official meeting of the commission in May 1866, they selected Galen Clark to be guardian. Clark, who was also one of the original commissioners, would serve a total of 22 years as guardian and become known as the most able, conscientious, and dedicated state guardian to serve at Yosemite.

In total, seven men, along with an equal number of deputies, would serve as state guardians or rangers at Yosemite from 1866 to 1906. In 1906, Yosemite Valley and the Mariposa Grove were returned to federal control to become part of the larger Yosemite National Park.

The return of Yosemite Valley to federal control in 1906 did not end the role of California state park rangers. In 1891, a guardian had been appointed at the recently established Marshall

Gold Discovery Monument at Coloma. His duties were the "care and protection of the Marshall Monument and grounds from vandalism and injury." The Marshall Gold Discovery site remains the oldest park in the current state park system. The first Marshall Monument guardian was Ezram M. Smith, a local Coloma businessman and rancher, who was paid $50 a month.

Another state historic park was established at Sutter's Fort in 1895, and William Todd was appointed as guardian. Little is known about the early Sutter's Fort guardians except that the second guardian was James A. White, appointed in 1903, and the third guardian was E. H. Cox Sr., who served from 1909 to 1913.

Finally, the California Redwood Park at Big Basin was established in 1902 by the efforts of Andrew P. Hill and the Sempervirens Club. Shortly after being established, the commission charged with managing the park selected J. H. B. Pilkington to be guardian. Pilkington had been the horticulture commissioner for Santa Cruz County. Pilkington was paid a starting salary of $125 per month. Shortly after his appointment, the "guardian" title was changed to "park warden." This title was used in all state parks until 1945, when the title "park ranger" was officially adopted.

Possibly the earliest recorded reference to the term "ranger" is found in the English Rolls of Parliament, dated 1455. This usage referred to a royal forest officer or gamekeeper appointed to patrol royal forests to prevent poaching and trespassing. The first use of the term "park ranger" occurred at the turn of the century when civilian forest agents hired by the federal government were referred to as "park rangers." Finally, in 1905, the term "park ranger" was officially adopted for use in the national parks in California.

"Guardian" and "sub-guardian" were the first titles used in California's state parks starting in 1866. Shortly after the turn of the century, the titles "warden," "assistant warden," and "deputy warden" replaced the guardian title. In the 1930s, a variety of field classification titles were being used. These included "park warden," "seasonal naturalist," "recreation leader," "custodian," and "superintendent." In 1945, the "state park ranger" title was officially adopted. Other titles used during this time include "ranger," "assistant ranger," "deputy ranger," "chief ranger," and "superintendent."

In the 1950s, a "park attendant" classification was created. Although park attendants' primary duties were maintenance, they also wore badges and did some visitor services work. As a practical matter, most park attendants promoted into the higher-paying ranger ranks. In 1970, all maintenance duties were removed from the ranger duty statement and a new set of pure maintenance classifications and positions were created. In the early days, field rangers did every job in the parks.

Today there is a team of dedicated and committed park staff working in the field and at the Sacramento headquarters. This staff includes rangers, facility and maintenance services workers, environmental scientists, interpreters, archeologists, planners, seasonal workers, volunteers, and administration staff.

From Galen Clark's time to the present day, rangers have faced the ongoing day-to-day job of protecting and preserving the state's outstanding natural and cultural areas, maintaining a safe environment for park visitors, and educating the public. They must do this while at the same time allowing for the widest possible public use and enjoyment of these areas. With over 76 million people a year visiting California's 270 state park units, the challenge for rangers is both daunting and multifaceted. However, for the last 140 years and into the future, this has and will be the proud and demanding job of California's state park rangers.

One

THE FIRST
PARK RANGERS
GUARDIANS OF YOSEMITE STATE PARK

Galen Clark's appointment as the first state guardian of Yosemite in May 1866 started 40 years of state park operation at Yosemite Valley and the Mariposa Grove of Big Trees.

Clark was an ideal choice for the guardian job. He was an outdoorsman and an early explorer of the Yosemite region. He is credited with being the first person not of Native American descent to discover the Mariposa Grove of Big Trees. His knowledge of the area was vast, and he was prominent in influencing those responsible for establishing Yosemite as a park.

Clark started work with an eight-page letter of instruction from the Yosemite board of commissioners. Among the instructions was the directive that he strictly enforce the new state laws enacted to protect the park. In addition, trails and bridges were to be kept in order. Clark was also given broad authority to "prevent either visitors and settlers from doing anything which would tend to impair the present picturesque appearance of the Valley." Clark was to also take charge of the Native Americans in Yosemite and to curb their practice of burning off large areas of the valley. Finally, Clark was to make sure that the early Yosemite settlers submitted to the authority of the commission. This duty was one that grew quite messy and drawn out. It took eight years and a decision of the U.S. Supreme Court to resolve the issue in favor of the authority of the guardian and commission.

Clark's assignment was daunting, but he was authorized to appoint a sub-guardian, or deputy ranger, to assist him. Clark named Yosemite Valley resident and pioneer Peter Longhurst as the first sub-guardian of Yosemite. The commission wanted Clark and Longhurst to be on duty at all times during the visitor season.

In total, seven men would serve as state guardians at Yosemite from 1866 to 1906. It was in 1906 that Yosemite Valley and the Mariposa Grove were returned to federal control to become part of Yosemite National Park. With more or less success, all the guardians faced the responsibility to protect the park, greet and educate the public, provide public facilities, maintain the peace, and generally administer the area.

Galen Clark was appointed state guardian of Yosemite on May 21, 1866. Clark was California's and the nation's first park ranger. Clark is pictured here on patrol near Nevada Falls. Just off this trail, Clark's Point was named after the first and most renowned guardian of Yosemite. Clark would serve two terms and a total of 22 years as guardian. (Courtesy of YNPRL.)

Galen Clark was an early explorer and homesteader in the Yosemite region. In 1855, he was among the earliest white men to enter Yosemite Valley. Clark is credited as being the first person not of Native American descent to discover the Mariposa Grove of Big Trees in 1857. This picture was taken in front of the Grizzly Giant in 1858 or 1859. (Courtesy of YNPRL; photograph by Carleton E. Watkins.)

On June 30, 1864, at the height of the Civil War, Pres. Abraham Lincoln took time to sign a bill that had glided through Congress with little fanfare. Carried by California Sen. John Conness, the bill provided that Yosemite Valley and the Mariposa Grove were "granted to the State of California . . . [with] the express condition that the premises shall be held for public use, resort and recreation . . . inalienable for all time." (Courtesy of the Library of Congress.)

As the new guardian, Galen Clark was given an eight-page letter of instruction regarding his duties. He was to protect and administer the new park, pacify Yosemite's Native Americans, strictly enforce the new state laws enacted to protect the park, and prepare the park for public use. Clark is pictured here with some of the many tourists who soon flocked to Yosemite. (Courtesy of YNPRL.)

Galen Clark was an active supporter of protecting Yosemite and the Mariposa Grove. After the enactment of federal legislation in 1864, Gov. Frederick F. Low immediately appointed Clark, Frederick Law Olmsted, and six others to a provisional Yosemite commission. Clark's days of lazing in the beauty of Yosemite Valley, as he is pictured here, would end with his appointment as guardian. (Courtesy of YNPRL.)

The Yosemite Native Americans also came under Clark's charge. He persuaded them to stop their annual burning of the valley. Restricting these "controlled" burns quickly caused the valley to become overgrown. Clark and later guardians would have to order large-scale cutting of brush to maintain the "picturesque appearance of the Valley." Pictured are Suzie and Sadie McGowan (Mono Lake Paiute Indians) in 1901. (Courtesy of YNPRL.)

One of Guardian Clark's early duties was to issue leases to those who had settled in Yosemite Valley before it had been set aside as a park. One such settler was George F. Leidig, seated (third from left) on the porch of his pre-park hotel. In 1868, Clark appointed Leidig to be sub-guardian or deputy ranger. (Courtesy of YNPRL.)

Guardian Galen Clark was a fearless and relentless explorer, both on foot and by horse. John Muir said Clark was "the best mountaineer I ever met." Clark is pictured here on the overhang rock at Glacier Point. As guardian, Clark had guardrails installed at Glacier Point for the safety of more timid visitors. (Courtesy of YNPRL.)

John Muir, founder of the Sierra Club, arrived in Yosemite Valley in 1868 and met Galen Clark, who was then the guardian. Muir and Clark shared a kinship and love of Yosemite. They made many exploration trips together. Muir wrote an extensive memorial to Clark upon his death in 1910, which included calling Clark "one of the most sincere tree-lovers I ever knew." (Courtesy of Shirley Sargent.)

Clark knew and befriended most of the famous photographers of Yosemite. This photograph is by friend and photographer Carleton Watkins, who maintained the Yosemite Art Gallery in San Francisco. This portrait of Clark was taken in the mid-1870s in San Francisco while Clark was attending a Yosemite Park Commission meeting. (Photograph by Carleton E. Watkins; courtesy of YNPRL.)

In 1875, the Yosemite Park Commission provided a home and office for guardian Galen Clark. This 10-foot-by-30-foot building became the very first ranger station, complete with a guardian sign over the door. (Courtesy of YNPRL.)

Yosemite's second guardian and California's second state park ranger was James M. Hutchings, appointed in September 1880. Hutchings had been one of the earliest discovers of Yosemite Valley and the first to publish and promote its beauty and splendor. Backed by a friendlier legislature, Hutchings was able to oversee many improvements at Yosemite, including the acquisition of toll roads and trails. (Courtesy of YNPRL.)

James Hutchings spent his whole life promoting Yosemite in books, lectures that he illustrated with lantern slides, and outings. Hutchings, fifth from the left in this picture, is seen leading a party at Yosemite. The group is in front of the Yosemite Chapel. (Photograph by George Fiske; Courtesy of YNPRL.)

The third Yosemite guardian was Walter E. Dennison, who served from 1885 to 1887. Dennison was a young engineer who had worked in mining and transportation. He had no special appreciation for Yosemite. He did oversee the construction of a new hotel in the valley and the Vernal Falls Bridge, which allowed a trail link between Nevada Falls and Glacier Point. (Courtesy of YNPRL.)

Mark McCord served as Yosemite guardian from 1887 to 1889. McCord was an employee of the powerful Southern Pacific Railroad Company with no particular qualifications for guardian. In less then two years, McCord was replaced after allegations of mismanagement, including cutting of timber for personal gain. After an extensive state senate investigation in 1889, McCord was fired. (Courtesy of YNPRL.)

An active 75-year-old Galen Clark was again appointed guardian in 1889. Clark's appointment was lauded in the local newspaper: "A more fitting appointment would be impossible. Mr. Clark knows how the visitors should be treated . . . He is a great lover of nature and will not permit natural beauties to be ruthlessly destroyed." Clark is seen here on patrol in the valley in 1891.

Guardian Clark (center) is pictured here with a group of park visitors at the Wawona Tree. During Clark's second term, visitor use increased dramatically. In 1895, Clark hired the first summer patrol officers or seasonal rangers to patrol the public campgrounds and enforce regulations. The use of seasonal rangers is a practice that has continued to this day in the park service. (Courtesy of CSP.)

After Galen Clark's retirement in 1897, the Yosemite Park Commission recognized Clark for "his faithful and eminent services as Guardian, his constant efforts to preserve, protect and enhance the beauties of Yosemite, his dignified, kindly and courteous demeanor to all . . . deserve from us a fitting recognition." Clark stayed on at Yosemite in a variety of capacities. In retirement, Clark wrote three small books, including *The Yosemite Valley* and *Indians of the Yosemite*.

Miles Wallace succeeded Galen Clark as guardian in 1897. Wallace, pictured here in front of the Grizzly Giant, had served as a district attorney in nearby Madera County. Wallace's two years in office, which ended in 1899, were fairly productive and positive. (Courtesy of YNPRL.)

The last Yosemite guardian was George Harlow, who replaced John Stevens. Stevens was guardian from 1899 to 1904. No photographs of Stevens are known to exist. Harlow (third from the left) is seen here in Yosemite Valley, probably in the winter of 1905. Second from the left is Harlow's wife, Stella. Harlow served from 1901 until Yosemite was returned to the federal government in 1906.

Pres. Theodore "Teddy" Roosevelt and John Muir rode through Yosemite Valley in 1903 during a camping and riding trip through the Yosemite area. This trip allowed Muir to convince President Roosevelt that Yosemite Valley and Mariposa Grove should be taken from state control and returned to the federal government to become part of the larger Yosemite National Park. In 1890, the "Yosemite Forest Reserve" had been set aside. Within a few years, the reserve began to be called Yosemite National Park. It took two years, but in 1906, the state era ended. On June 11, 1906, President Roosevelt signed a bill returning Yosemite Valley and the Mariposa Grove to federal control to become the heart of Yosemite National Park. (Photograph by Southern Pacific Railroad; courtesy of YNPRL.)

With the transfer of state control of Yosemite Valley to the federal government in 1906, the U.S. Army Cavalry, who patrolled Yosemite National Park, moved their headquarters to the valley. It was not until 1916 that the National Park Service was formed and civilian park rangers began administering and protecting Yosemite.

In 1916, the National Park Service (NPS) was formed, and civilian rangers took over the protection and administration of Yosemite. NPS rangers Billy Nelson (left) and Jim Lloyd pose in front of the early Yosemite ranger station. Notice the sign between them that reads, "When in Doubt Ask a Ranger." (Courtesy of YNPRL.)

Two

RANGERS IN
THE EARLY PARKS
1891–1928

In 1891, forty-niner Ezram Smith was appointed guardian at the recently established Marshall Gold Discovery Monument at Coloma. Smith served as guardian until 1896 and was succeeded by Philip Truscher.

Another state historic park was established at Sutter's Fort in 1895, and William Todd was appointed guardian. Little is known about the early Sutter's Fort guardians except that the second guardian was James A. White, appointed in 1903.

The California Redwood Park at Big Basin was established in 1902 by the efforts of the Sempervirens Club. J. H. B. Pilkington was appointed as Big Basin guardian and shortly afterwards, in 1903, the position was retitled as warden. Pilkington was paid a salary of $125 per month. The title "park warden" would be used until 1945.

The major event during Pilkington's term was the fire of 1904. Working under the direction of Warden Pilkington, volunteer firefighting crews were successful in saving the trees and buildings in the main area of the park.

The next Big Basin warden was Sam Rambo, appointed in 1907. At that time, Big Basin was operated under state forester Gerald B. Lull. In 1911, Rambo gained the dubious distinction of becoming the first park warden to be fired. Rambo, along with his boss, Lull, authorized the cutting of live redwood trees for commercial gain. Lull, for his part, was forced from office.

William H. "Billy" Dool replaced Rambo in 1911. Dool had a 20-year career as warden. Because of his personal example, his energy, and his many accomplishments, Dool is considered the best of the early wardens and the person who professionalized the ranger job. Serving under Dool were several deputies, including C. A. Reed, Joseph Park, Elmer Crawford, Charlie Lewis, and Fred Canham.

Finally, in the 1920s, through the efforts of the Save-the-Redwoods League and others, several redwood parks were established. These included Humboldt Redwoods, Prairie Creek Redwoods, and Richardson Grove Redwoods. The first rangers at Humboldt Redwoods were Solon Williams and G. E. Thompson, who where "State Foresters" working for the State Board of Forestry. In 1928, Thompson would become the park warden of Humboldt Redwoods State Park.

The Marshall Gold Discovery Monument was dedicated on May 3, 1890, becoming California's first state historic park. In 1891, the legislature authorized the governor to appoint a guardian to protect the monument and grounds from vandalism and injury. A total of six guardians would serve at the Marshall Monument from 1891 to 1928, when it became part of the Division of Parks. (Courtesy of CSP.)

The first guardian or ranger at the Marshall Gold Discovery Monument was Ezram "Cow" Smith, pictured here with his wife. Smith served as guardian from June 24, 1891, to September 14, 1896. Smith had earned the nickname "Cow" because he had operated the first commercial dairy in Coloma, California. Later guardians included German immigrant Francis Truscher (1866–1896) and Francis Nichols (1899–1903).

In 1948, a huge 100th anniversary celebration was held at the Marshall Gold Discovery State Historic Park to commemorate the discovery of gold in California. Rangers can be seen in this picture sprucing up the monument for the big event. (Courtesy of CSP.)

Sutter's Fort in Sacramento was opened to the public in 1893, becoming the state's second historic park. The historic Mexican-era fort had become very run down, and the primary job of the initial guardian was to protect it from further destruction. The man sitting on the porch in this picture appears to be wearing a badge, and it would be nice to think he is William Todd, the fort's first guardian.

The California Redwood Park at Big Basin was established in 1902. The entrance sign proclaims: "To be preserved in a state of nature." The park would be the largest and most heavily staffed park in the system well into the 1940s. In 1928, half of all permanent wardens (rangers) in the Division of Parks worked at Big Basin. (Courtesy of the Sempervirens Fund; photograph by F. Roy Fulmer.)

The first warden appointed at the California Redwood Park was J. Humphrey B. Pilkington. He served from 1903 to 1907 Pilkington is shown here in 1904 or 1905 seated at the first and very modest public campfire center. (Courtesy of CSP.)

By 1919, the public campfire center had grown dramatically in size from its humble beginnings seen in the previous picture. Wardens, and later seasonal naturalists and recreation leaders, would give evening programs in the summer on park features and activities, natural history, and even provide some entertainment for the visiting public. At the time of this picture, William Dool was warden. (Photograph by A. H. Johannsen.)

In 1907, state forester Gerald B. Lull was made administrator of the California Redwood State Park. Lull appointed Sam Rambo as park warden. Both would eventually be subject to allegations of mismanagement, including authorizing the commercial harvesting of redwood trees in the park. In 1911, because of their actions, a new governor abruptly replaced both Lull and Rambo.

William H. "Billy" Dool became warden at Big Basin in 1911. He is pictured here sometime after 1917 wearing the first known state park badge. Dool would serve as warden for 20 years. He was the best known of the early state park wardens and the person who first "professionalized" the park ranger job. (Courtesy of CSP.)

Joseph Park is pictured here wearing one of the earliest known state park badges. Park served as assistant warden from 1915 to 1934. He was described as "of fine character, quiet and efficient, he made many friends among the employees as well as the thousands of visitors to the Big Basin."

Assistant warden Joseph P. Park patrols through the Big Basin State Redwood Park sign in the 1920s. The small signs to the left of Park's vehicle read, "Do Not Pick Flowers or Shrubs" and "Do Not Build Fires." Protection of the park and enforcement of park rules and other laws were a constant duty for wardens.

A longtime deputy warden at Big Basin was Fred Canham, seen in this postcard "calling in the deer." This was a summer attraction at Big Basin where the ranger would call in the deer for feeding each evening. The show was so popular that a number of different postcards were made and sold showing various rangers "calling in the deer." (Photograph by F. Roy Fulmer.)

Deputy warden Albert M. Weaver can be seen here wearing his park badge in the 1920s. The box he carries contains food for the deer. This picture is probably by Andrew P. Hill, park photographer at Big Basin in the 1920s. (Courtesy of CSP.)

Andrew P. Hill was an early advocate for the establishment of Big Basin as a park. Hill was a well-known San Francisco Bay Area photographer who founded the Sempervirens Club to promote saving Big Basin as a park. Hill later had a photography shop in the park, and in 1911 was an unsuccessful candidate for park warden. (Courtesy of CSP.)

This is an early image of the warden's office at Big Basin. Besides being the public information center of the park, it also served as the post office and stage stop. (Courtesy of the Sempervirens Fund.)

By 1934, the warden's office at Big Basin had been enlarged and improved with a small visitors center. Standing at the window is warden Fred O. Moody. One can just barely make out the star badge on his vest. Moody served as warden from 1934 to 1937. Before becoming warden, he had worked for the Boulder Creek-Big Basin Stage Line owned by his father, J. J. Moody.

Richardson Grove State Park was one of the many redwood parks established in the 1920s by the efforts of the Save-the-Redwoods League. The warden's office was right on the Redwood Highway and easily accessible to the public. This picture dates from the 1930s. The park was named for California's 25th governor, William F. Richardson.

Humboldt Redwoods State Park was established in the 1920s, primarily through the efforts of the State Board of Forestry. The Board of Forestry operated and staffed the park with two state forest rangers until 1928 when it became part of the Division of Parks.

The first two state forest rangers at Humboldt Redwoods were Solon Williams (No. 19) and G. E. Thompson (No. 22), shown in this 1921 group picture. The State Board of Forestry administered Humboldt until 1928. G. E. Thompson was Williams's assistant. In 1928, the park was transferred from state forestry to Division of Parks control. Thompson moved with it and became the first park warden. (Courtesy of California Department of Forestry and Fire Protection.)

Newton Drury was a towering figure in the park movement, both in California and the nation. In 1919, he became the first executive director of the Save-the-Redwoods League, responsible for the establishment of many of the early redwood parks. Drury would later serve as director of the National Park Service and chief of the California Division of Beaches and Parks from 1951 to 1959. (Courtesy of CSP.)

Another outstanding figure in the park movement was Joseph R. Knowland (left). In 1921, Knowland was appointed to the Mount Diablo State Park Commission and actively served over 20 years on the California State Park and Recreation Commission, starting in the 1930s. Knowland was made an honorary state park ranger in 1964. The first woman state park commissioner, Mrs. Edmund N. "Madie" Brown (right) and commissioner P. F. Hatch (center) are also in this 1934 picture.

Three

DIVISION OF PARKS
1928–1945

Major changes in the ranger service occurred with the formal establishment of the Division of Parks in the Department of Natural Resources on January 1, 1928. All the formerly independently operated state parks and rangers were put under the supervision of the chief of the new division. The first chief was Charles B. Wing of Palo Alto.

There were only 17 permanent personnel, mainly rangers, working about a dozen state parks in 1928. In some of the early parks, like Burney Falls and Mount Diablo, there were no rangers assigned to them at all.

In this same year, the public also passed a large state park bond act. A great expansion of the park system ensued. By 1938, this expansion had resulted in the Division of Parks growing threefold to over 50 permanent personnel and a number of seasonal employees.

The first women rangers were hired during this era. Most notable of the early women in state parks was Harriet "Petey" Weaver, who started working at Big Basin Redwoods in 1930. Petey, an author and teacher, would work for 20 years and retired in 1950 with deputy ranger badge number 105. Another early women ranger was Clara B. Morrill, who served three years at Marshall Gold Discovery State Historic Park starting in 1932.

The first uniforms were authorized in 1940. Before this, rangers had badges but no official uniform. Many historical ranger pictures can be dated as being either before or after 1940 because of the uniform factor.

The rangers during this era were real jack-of-all-trades, responsible for every aspect of the park operation, including a variety of visitor services, protection work, facility upkeep, trail building, and much more.

World War II would bring many changes to the ranger ranks, as it did to most of the rest of society at that time. Ranger staffing levels and budgets were slashed, and park visitation was very low during the war years. One significant change that occurred in 1945 was that the park warden title was officially changed to "state park ranger."

The first ranger chief was Charles B. Wing. Wing had been an activist in the park movement, including the establishment of the California Redwood Park at Big Basin in 1902, and had served for many years on the Redwood Park Commission. A longtime park advocate, Wing oversaw a major expansion of the ranger ranks and new parks. Wing served as chief until 1934.

It is thought that this is deputy warden William Kenyon standing next to the vehicle in front of the Big Basin warden's office in 1936. Kenyon would work his way up through the ranks to what is today called division chief. The California Redwood Park at Big Basin had the largest number of rangers and was the most developed and visited park in the 1930s.

Ranger Harvey W. Moore gives a ride to what appears to be Girl Scouts. This 1936 Cuyamaca State Park picture was taken before rangers had official uniforms. (Courtesy of CSP.)

This is a drawing of a brawny, idealized park warden and superintendent as they appeared on the 1928 Division of Parks organizational chart. (Courtesy of CSP.)

Deputy park warden Jess T. Chaffee is seen here in the 1930s at Pfeiffer Redwoods State Park with his version of a uniform. High boots, riding pants, and the official badge seemed to be a part of the uniform look that developed at that time. (Courtesy of CSP.)

This group of rangers was gathered at Big Basin Redwoods for an all-employee conference in 1938. One topic of the conference was developing standardized uniforms. As pictured, there were some great differences in the unofficial uniforms worn by rangers at the time. From left to right are Everett Powell, Bill Kenyon, Alfred P. Salzgeber, Clyde L. Newlin, Earl Hanson, and Leo Fry.

This is a picture of ranger Leo Fry standing with the "wild" deer at Big Basin in 1940. Fry is in the first ranger uniform, adopted the same year. The Big Basin ranger station can be partially seen behind the redwood tree. (Photograph by F. Roy Fulmer.)

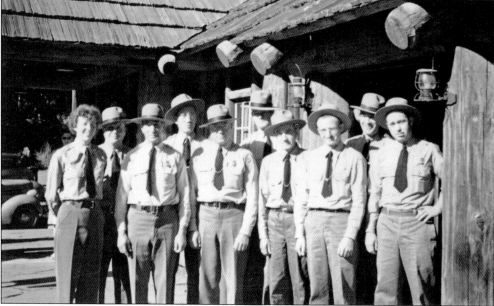

Considered the first woman ranger, Harriett E. "Petey" Weaver stands out in this picture of Big Basin rangers in 1945. They are, from left to right, Harriett E. Weaver, Arlan Sholes, Charles H. Fakler, Melville Whittaker, C. L. "Roy" Cushing, William A. Weatherbee, Floyd C. "Carl" Saddlemyre, Arthur Parvin, Darrell A. Knoefler, and Louis Donaldson. Weaver started work in 1930 and retired in 1950 with deputy ranger badge number 105.

The campfire center at Big Basin Redwood Park was one of the largest and most heavily used in the park system in the 1940s. Rangers and seasonal naturalists gave nightly programs on the weekends and other days during the summer months. Harriett "Petey" Weaver is at the microphone, with ranger Arlan Sholes backstage, perhaps waiting to make his appearance.

Harriett E. "Petey" Weaver is holding Frosty the raccoon. Weaver adopted Frosty while working at Big Basin Redwood Park. Weaver's experience with Frosty led her to write a popular children's book titled *Frosty: a Raccoon to Remember*. Weaver is wearing the first state park patch authorized in 1940. Weaver was the author of nine other books and wrote for *Sunset* for 30 years.

John H. "Jack" Knight is seen here with his wife, Barbara, at Mount Diablo State Park around 1940. Knight would become one of the most well-known rangers and administrators in the postwar and modern park eras. Starting as a seasonal employee in 1937, Knight rose through the ranks working at virtually every level. He served over 40 years and retired in 1980 as associate director for operations.

Ranger Albert A. Beck feeds an orphan deer at Calaveras Big Trees State Park around 1943. Then and now, rangers have a responsibility for the protection and care of wildlife in the parks. By 1948, Beck had been promoted to Columbia State Historic Park.

This cover of the *California Conservationist* from 1940 featured an unidentified ranger on ski patrol at D. L. Bliss State Park at Lake Tahoe. John W. Calvert was the Lake Tahoe ranger at the time. There are now several state parks at Lake Tahoe, and rangers still patrol on skis and lead ski hikes in the area. The *California Conservationist* was the official publication of the California Department of Natural Resources.

By 1943, Gordon T. Kishbaugh was the ranger at D. L. Bliss State Park at Lake Tahoe. Here is Kishbaugh's loaded 1941 Willys park truck and trailer at Ebbetts Pass hauling the family from Tahoe to Calaveras Big Trees State Park for the winter. For many years, the Tahoe park staff would move and work in another park during the winter months.

Ranger Gordon T. Kishbaugh is cleaning up a downed tree and splitting the wood for park use at D. L. Bliss State Park. In the early days, most rangers lived in the parks, often under primitive conditions. These living conditions and duties helped maintain the ranger image of someone who was paid to "hunt, fish and live in a log cabin" as part of their job.

An unidentified ranger leads park visitors on a hike at Lake Tahoe in the 1940s. Conducting campfire programs, leading hikes, and providing park natural history information were a regular part of the ranger job. Many of these activities started out in a very simple and informal way. By the 1940s, these activities evolved into larger and more formal park programs.

Ranger Alvin F. Whittington is getting ready for late patrol at Big Sur State Park in the mid-1940s. The patrol sedan has a "Division of Parks" door decal, first adopted around 1940.

Assistant ranger Lloyd Lively is shown with two semi-tame orphaned bears at Big Sur State Park in 1940. Even during this time, rangers would not ordinarily have wild animal shows for park visitors. It is not known exactly why the bears were being kept. Most likely, once they grew older, they were released into the wild.

In 1945, Mount Diablo State Park had only two rangers. Pictured are rangers William E. Gott (left) and William J. Reinhardt. Reinhardt was a brand new ranger in 1945 and looks it in this picture.

Richardson Grove Redwoods was very popular in the 1930s but had fewer visitors during World War II. The warden's office was located right next to the Redwood Highway that ran through the park. On the right side of the picture, an unidentified ranger can be seen standing on the porch of the warden's office.

District Superintendents

PERCY FRENCH GUY FLEMING LEE BLAISDELL EVERETT POWELL BOB COON JACK KNIGHT

1928 – 1980

BILL KENYON JESS CHAFFEE GEORGE HOLMBOE CLYDE NEWLIN JIM WARREN GORDON KISHBAUGH

JIM TRYNER TINY PHILBROOK BOB HATCH JIM WHITEHEAD LLOYD LIVELY BILL HAESSLER DICK BROCK

CARL ANDERSON CURT MITCHELL TED WILSON WALT FRINKE HERB HEINZE RON McCULLOUGH JOHN MICHAEL KEITH CALDWELL

Kingpins of the early state park operations

The "District Superintendents" were kingpins of state park operations from 1928-1980's. By the 1970's, the state was divided up into six Districts, each headed up by a District Superintendent. In 1980's, these positions were replaced by "Regional Directors" and later on by the three "Division Chiefs" of today. 25 years later, there is little other information or even other photos of many of these early state park operation kingpins. Doug Bryce produced this collage.

District superintendents were the kingpins of early state park operations. In 1928, two superintendents split up the whole state. Eventually the state was divided into six districts, each headed up by a district superintendent. "Regional directors," and later the "division chiefs" of today, replaced the superintendent positions in the 1980s. Douglas R. Bryce, who started his career as a ranger in 1957, produced this poster. (Courtesy of CSP.)

On V-J Day in August 1945, rangers sounded the siren at the Big Basin ranger station, and park visitors flocked to hear the good news that World War II was over. The end of the war and the prosperity that followed would lead to a great increase in state park use and heralded a large expansion of the state park system.

Four

THE POSTWAR RANGERS
1946–1969

The end of World War II opened up the ranger ranks as visitation soared and new parks were added to the system. In the five years following the war, field staff positions jumped from 100 to nearly 250. This expansion would continue until the 1960s.

At the beginning of this era, rangers were still jack-of-all trades doing every job in the field. However, change was coming in the form of specialization. First the department started hiring more seasonal employees. In the late 1940s and 1950s, this included seasonal naturalists and recreation leaders. These summer employees took over and expanded the education and interpretation work like campfire programs and leading guided hikes. The next big change came in 1956 when the park attendant classification was introduced. This was the first maintenance worker position established in the field and was the harbinger of the end of maintenance duties by rangers. This transition was made complete in 1970.

Ranger pay was still low, and rangers worked a six-day, 48-hour week with no overtime pay until 1948. Real improvements in pay and premium credit for overtime would not come for decades. Low pay and hard work was a very applicable description for rangers during this period.

By the 1960s, more changes were on the way. Crime, heavy use, and overuse became issues demanding more of many rangers' time. Established duties in traditional parks far from cities and city problems were being overshadowed by the demands of newer high-use, high-recreation parks and beaches near big population centers. Heavy visitor use meant more people work for rangers, including enforcement, rescue, and medical aid.

The 1960s were a time of change in California society and in the ranger service. Most traditional ranger duties continued through the 1960s, perhaps with a changed emphasis. However, by the end of the decade, the many changes and pressures affecting the parks would bring about a fundamental change in the ranger job, producing the modern professional ranger known today.

The end of World War II brought home many family members serving in the military, including the son or grandson of ranger Al Beck at Calaveras Big Trees State Park. Many rangers had gone off to war, and when the war was over, many returned to their old park jobs.

In addition to personnel returning from duty in World War II, the parks also acquired, or were the recipients of, military surplus equipment. Calaveras Big Trees, like many parks in the system, got military surplus jeeps to use as patrol vehicles, such as this one driven by ranger Al Beck.

Ranger Jack Knight checks in a visitor at Calaveras Big Trees State Park in 1946. The end of World War II and renewed prosperity brought visitors back into the parks starting in the summer of 1946. Notice the young admirer on the left side of the picture. Jack Knight was a famous figure within the park service. He served over 40 years in state parks and retired as a deputy director.

Speaking of postwar crowds, this campfire program at Richardson Grove State Park has an unidentified ranger making a presentation to over 200 people! Starting in the 1950s, more seasonal rangers and other seasonal summer staff were used. These seasonal naturalists and recreation leaders were hired in the bigger parks to lead hikes and do campfire programs.

Here is one of the first training sessions conducted for seasonal naturalists, who provided guided walks, campfire, and other visitor programs during the summer months. Newton Drury, chief of the division, is in the center of the group wearing a light jacket. Those wearing badges in this picture are rangers, and the others are naturalists. Although they had naturalist titles, most park visitors probably thought of them as seasonal rangers.

This is a busy Ventura State Beach about 1951. Starting in the early 1940s, the state embarked on a program to acquire more state beaches. These high use beaches, often close to cities, changed the type of work rangers were required to do, including more public safety responsibilities. With the increase in visitors, more park rangers and other staff were also needed and hired.

Lifeguard Michael Henry (left) and an unidentified ranger look over the numerous visitors at Carpinteria State Beach. The state park lifeguard service was established in 1950. Initially, lifeguards performed rescues and medical aid while rangers did the other visitor services work on state beaches. More recently, permanent lifeguards (who are full state peace officers) oversee rescue, medical aid, law enforcement, and other visitor services operations at many state beaches.

Robert J. "Bob" Isenor was hired as the first state park lifeguard in 1950. He is considered the father of the state park lifeguard service. Isenor was responsible for building the lifeguard program. He was instrumental in many improvements, including covered lifeguard towers, rescue boats, and dispatch services. Isenor passed away on June 6, 2000, and his ashes were scattered at sea off Huntington State Beach.

After World War II and into the 1960s, the rapid expansion of the park system included not only beaches, but also many new parks and a new type of park—state recreation areas. As seen in this 1960 picture of the Folsom Lake State Recreation Area, the new recreational parks attracted large crowds and a corresponding workload for rangers. A 1950s Ford sedan patrol car is visible in the left front side of this photograph.

Warden J. Dana Staiger and his family are shown here at Sea Cliff State Beach in the 1940s. They lived in a park house right next to the main parking area, available day and night for visitor needs. Most rangers and their families lived in the parks during this era. The whole family would often be involved in the park in one way or another, even if just to answer questions or call for help. (Courtesy of David Albrecht.)

Several unidentified park spouses and kids pose on the entrance road into the new housing area at Big Basin in the 1950s. By the 1970s, it was no longer practical or economically feasible to provide park housing for all park staff. However, even today almost all parks still have some residences and at least one or more houses where rangers are required to live in the park for 24-hour protection.

Rangers in the 1940s and 1950s were real jacks-of-all-trades. As shown in this late 1940s picture of Pfeiffer Big Sur, they were expected to provide all services at the park, from checking in visitors to supplying firewood. During the summer months, the rangers concentrated on visitor-related duties, including patrol, campground operations, and even the more mundane jobs of cleaning restrooms and picking up litter. During the winter, off-season rangers were expected to do everything necessary to keep the park operating, including repairs, construction, and maintenance.

Ranger Bob Hiller works on the water system at the Vikingsholm in D. L. Bliss State Park in 1953. It was not until the 1960s that state parks created formal maintenance worker positions responsible for day-to-day maintenance, new construction, and upkeep of park facilities. (Courtesy of CSP.)

Ranger Jack Lemley cleans up the restroom sinks at Calaveras Big Trees State Park in the 1940s. For rangers, no matter how their duty statement might read, there was always a final line stating "and other duties as required." (Courtesy of CSP.)

Although rangers had bigger crowds and more work, there was still the requirement to explore and know every square inch of their park. Ranger William Kenyon is doing just that as he sits on top of Mount San Jacinto Peak in the 1950s. The heavily carved-up sign in the picture says the elevation is 10,805 feet, but a more modern source puts the peak at 10,834 feet. (Courtesy of CSP.)

Four unidentified rangers are exploring deep within the caves at Mitchell Caverns State Park in 1955. Two of the rangers in this picture might be Orville Short, the park supervisor, and Walter G. Palmer, the assistant supervisor.

Anza-Borrego Desert State Park is the largest park in the system with over half a million acres. Ranger Carl G. Wakefield is seen here at Palm Canyon in Borrego. It was reported that "duty in this park is truly an inspiring one . . . Daily rangers are finding things hitherto unknown." Another note stated: "[we] are also hopeful of getting a two-way radio system soon."

In 1957, Borrego had 12 rangers, 1 park attendant, and 1 park naturalist to administer, maintain, patrol, and protect this very large—over 500,000 acres—park. A 1957 department newsletter article about the Borrego rangers stated that "the duties of the State Park Rangers stationed in the . . . park are not generally known to other men in the field. Much of their work is patrol with jeeps to protect state park lands."

From the start of the park system, wildlife protection has been one of the primary ranger duties. An unidentified ranger checks out a group of desert tortoises at Anza-Borrego Desert State Park. Because of their value as pets, tortoises are a constant target of wildlife thieves. (Courtesy of CSP.)

Rangers are constantly assisting the public in numerous ways, like towing this visitor's car out of the snow at Calaveras Big Trees in 1960. The ranger's vehicle is a four-wheel-drive Willys Jeep with chains on all four wheels allowing it to go anywhere in the snow.

Almost every year in the 1950s and 1960s state parks had a large display staffed by rangers at the California State Fair. Here ranger Wesley Cater assists fair visitors with park information. Public information and natural/cultural history education are all still on the ranger duty statement. To this day, state parks normally has an information booth at the state fair each year. (Courtesy of CSP.)

An unidentified ranger makes an arrest. In the 1960s, all was not well in the parks. With increased use and more parks located near urban centers, crime had risen dramatically. Rangers had to perform more and more law enforcement duties without adequate training or equipment. A 1969 watershed investigation titled *Crime in the State Park System* set in motion major changes in the law enforcement role of the ranger.

After a long day in the park, ranger Gordon Kishbaugh is obviously looking forward to taking his boots off, at least for a few minutes. Kishbaugh is at the Calaveras Big Trees ranger office in 1947. Behind Kishbaugh is a crank phone that was used to connect the entrance station to the ranger office in case of emergencies or needed instructions. This crank phone system was a state-of-the-art communication system used at most larger parks at the time. It was not until the 1960s that two-way radios started to be used in the park system, and it was not until the late 1980s that a regular public-safety radio dispatch system was initiated for rangers in the field

Five

RANGER INSIGNIA
HATS, UNIFORMS, BADGES, AND PATCHES

The Smokey Bear hat is probably the most recognized ranger symbol. This was not always the case, as rangers did not even have official uniforms until 1939. The hat, also often referred to as a campaign or flat hat, is known in state parks as the Stetson. The name comes from John B. Stetson, who was a famous hat maker who made what was originally called the "boss of the plains."

In the beginning, it was not uniforms but badges that were issued as symbols of ranger authority. Although Yosemite state guardians had police powers and made arrests, there is no known evidence that they had or used badges. The first known official badges were issued to park wardens at the California Redwood Park in 1917. Since then, a variety of badges have been authorized.

Approved in 1939, the first official state park uniforms were debuted in 1940. They consisted of gray-green trousers and jacket, a gray shirt, black tie, and a stiff-brim Stetson campaign hat colored "Belgian Belly." With many changes over the years, today's uniform consists of green pants and jacket, tan shirt, green tie, and the Stetson-style campaign hat now made primarily by the Stratton Company.

With the new uniform, the first state park shoulder patch was also authorized. The patch was a 2-inch-by-4-inch semicircle with a California poppy design in the center, lettered "State Parks–California." In 1947, another semicircle patch, with a golden bear in the center, was brought into service.

A major change occurred in 1964, when a full 4-inch round patch was adopted. This also had a bear in the center and was lettered, "California State Park System." Since 1964, various round patches have been used. The current patch, in blue, green, and bright gold, is very distinctive and is sometimes called the "Hollywood" patch. In addition to shoulder patches, various hat and badge patches have been authorized and/or worn by rangers. A good detailed history of state park insignia is contained in the book *Insignia of the California Resources Agency*.

The second all-employee conference in 1940 at Big Sur featured the first official ranger uniform. Adopted in 1939, the uniform was gray-green in color with black leather and the Stetson flat hat. Most of the uniform has changed, but the Stetson ranger hat has remained a constant. The state park staff pictured are, from left to right (first row), Darwin Tate, Van Hall, Earl Hanson, Jack Covington, Otis Wilton, Bob Coon, Percy French, Ernie Camper, and Fred Perl; (second row)

Jack Fleckenstein, Jack Calvert, Ross Greely, Clyde Newlin, Ray Bassett, Charles Fakler, Guy Flemming, Jess Chafee, Lee Blaisdell, Fred Canham, Eugene Velyzy, Ted Milne, and Harvey More; (third row) Bob Boughey, Bill Kenyon, Murrell Gregory, Wilhemina Fakler, Louise Morley, Dana Staiger, Grace Gregory, John H. Knight, Barbara Knight, Ruby Coon, Marvis Walker, Harold Pesch, Leo Fry, and Roy Cushing.

The first known official badges were authorized for the warden and his deputies at the California Redwood Park in 1917. The warden's badge appears to be a large (maybe 3-inch to 3.5-inch) shield with a state of California center seal. The lettering "WARDEN" can be seen in the bottom rocker of the badge. Albert E. Weaver is wearing a warden badge sometime in the 1920s.

With the formation of the Division of Parks in 1928, a new 2.5-inch six-point ball-tip star with red enamel was introduced. This style was also used by state parks' sister agencies, the Division of Forestry (with green enamel) and the Division of Fish and Game (with blue enamel). Ranger William L. Kenyon is wearing his state park star sometime before uniforms were mandated in 1939.

Ranger Louis Wakefield is wearing the shield badge introduced in 1945. It was at this same time that the warden title was changed to ranger. The new badge was a 2.4-inch-by-1.75-inch shield with various titles on the top rocker. Titles included ranger, assistant ranger, deputy ranger, superintendent, and commissioner.

Ranger Burgess Heacox is wearing the 1953 badge. The previous shield badge was not very popular and many field rangers wanted to return to the star badge. In an effort to "make everyone happy," the 1953 shield included a five-point star in its center seal. With a name change to the Department of Parks and Recreation in 1961, the shield badge was modified with the new name.

Harriett E. "Petey" Weaver is wearing the 1945 badge and the first state park patch called the poppy patch. The poppy patch had been authorized in 1940, but probably due to the scarcity of uniform material during World War II, very few examples of it are still in existence. Weaver is considered the first woman ranger and served from 1930 to 1950.

In 1972, because of major changes in the ranger classification and their law enforcement authority, a new 2.8-inch, silver-colored star badge was issued. Similar to the 1928 badge, the new star was well received by the troops at the time. Ranger Lyle Watson is wearing the 1972 badge, the 1964 version patch, and four service stars on his left sleeve, representing 20 years of service.

Ranger James Burke is wearing the 1985 issue badge. He is holding an illegal firearm just seized in a marijuana raid in the northern redwoods. In the early 1980s, the State Park Peace Officers Association of California was pushing for a change in wording on the ranger badge. In 1984, the department agreed to change the wording from "State Park System" to "State Park Peace Officer."

In 1991, rangers celebrated 125 years of service and dedication to California's state parks and its citizens. The celebration was the brainchild of author Michael Lynch, who coordinated two years of anniversary events. Lynch is pictured here in 1990 wearing the anniversary badge he designed. Behind and to the right of Lynch is ranger Joseph Mette. In 1996, Lynch authored a book titled *Rangers of California's State Parks*.

This Resources Agency's gold six-point star was authorized for wear to commemorate California's 150-year statehood anniversary in 2000. Approved personnel in the State Departments of Parks, Fish and Game, and Forestry wore the badge. The badge was designed and developed by, from left to right, game warden Doug Messer, forestry fire captain Steve Huntington, and park ranger and author Michael Lynch.

This is one of several styles of badges worn by the state parks' K-9 patrol dogs. Bax, a German shepherd patrol dog worked by ranger Dave Berry, wore this badge. The department has had a K-9 program since 1969. Currently, there are about 14 canine handlers working throughout the state.

Shown are the proposed badge and patch for the 40th anniversary of the state parks' K-9 program to be celebrated in 2009. These represent just one part of a project to highlight and celebrate the accomplishments and history of the K-9 program that began with one canine handler, Dick Edwards, in 1969.

During the 1980s, the California State Park and Recreation Commission and Post Cereals developed a promotional campaign using a mascot called Cali the Quail. Cali never reached the popularity of Smokey Bear, but the Cali costumes, made by the Disney Company for about $5,000 each, did include a very large 6.5-inch badge. The Cali badge was the largest official state park badge ever produced.

This state park badge has quite a strange history. It was issued in 1939 to Fr. F. J. Caffery, who served on the California State Park and Recreation Commission for two years. In 1969, the badge was turned in to the Santa Monica Police Department, who returned it to the department. The now 74-year-old Caffery said that he carried the badge from 1939 until it went missing a few months before being returned.

In June 2002, Hollywood actor Clint Eastwood was sworn in as a California State Park Commissioner. After his swearing in ceremony, Eastwood held up his commission badge and told the crowd, "You're all under arrest." Eastwood served as an active and committed member of the commission until 2008 when he ran afoul of another Hollywood actor, Gov. Arnold Schwarzenegger, over a proposed freeway project through a state park.

There have been a wide variety of state park cloth badge patches developed and worn over the years. The patches have been used on ball caps, equipment, uniforms, and off-highway patrol riding outfits.

These are the main state park ranger patches worn over the years. From left to right, top to bottom, the patches are: poppy patch, 1940 to 1947, 4-inch-by-2-inch; golden bear patch, 1947 to 1964, 4-inch-by-2-inch; brown bear patch, 1964 to 1978, 4-inch; blazer patch, 1970s, 3-inch-by-4-inch; park system patch, 1978 to 1998, 4-inch; park system small patch, 1978 to 1998, 3-inch; state parks small patch, 1998 to 2005, 3-inch; state parks small patch, 1998 to 2005, 4-inch; and blue patch, 2005 to current, 4-inch.

Looking sharp in their Stetson ranger hats, ties, and Beaches and Parks patches are, from left to right, Murrell Gregory, Nelson Gerhard, and Chet Boyle. The three rangers were working at Calaveras Big Trees State Park when this picture was taken on January 24, 1948. (Courtesy of CSP)

In 1983, a centerfold-type picture appeared in an established fishing magazine. Although the state park patch was partially covered and the hat and badge were incorrect, the centerfold was considered demeaning to the ranger service. Both the State Park Peace Officers Association of California and California State Parks sent letters of protest to the magazine publisher. The protests seemed to have worked, as no new "ranger" centerfolds were published.

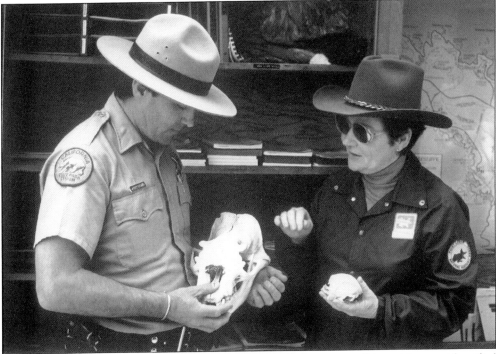

Ranger Gerald Loomis, left, is wearing the 1978-style patch. Loomis is talking with an unidentified state park volunteer from the Point Lobos Natural History Association (PLNHA) who provides public programs in the park. Note the volunteer is wearing a PLNHA patch on her left arm. (Photograph by Patricia Clark-Gray.)

In 2005, a new state park patch was approved. Ranger Nicole Van Doren is wearing the new design, which is based on the logo introduced in 2001 as part of a new branding program. Van Doren is seen here cutting down a marijuana plant during a raid in Humboldt Redwoods in 2006. (Courtesy of Richard Bergstreeser.)

Six

VINTAGE POSTCARDS
RANGERS AND PARKS

There is a wide variety of ranger and ranger-related vintage postcards. There are even greater numbers of historic and vintage postcards of parks themselves. Yosemite probably tops the list with the greatest number of postcards, numbering in the hundreds if not thousands.

It is probably because of the popularity of Yosemite postcards that cards of Galen Clark, first guardian of Yosemite, are the most numerous of the ranger postcards. Clark had a long career as guardian and was a Yosemite figure for even longer. He was a friend of—or was familiar with—most of the early Yosemite photographers. There are dozens of different postcards with Clark in them. Some of these cards were produced into the 1950s, and reprints of many Clark cards are still on sale today at Yosemite.

The California Redwood Park at Big Basin had its own park photography shop and park photographer starting in the 1930s. Correspondingly, there are quite a few Big Basin ranger postcards in existence. Both the Big Basin and Yosemite ranger postcards can still be found at postcard collector shows, sometimes even at a reasonable price.

The first Yosemite state guardian or ranger was Galen Clark, pictured here on a stereo view card at the Mariposa Grove sometime after 1866. Before he was appointed guardian, Clark was an early pioneer in Wawona and is credited with being the first person not of Native American descent to discover the Mariposa Grove of Big Trees. The double pictures on stereo cards gave them a 3-D effect when seen through a special viewer. (Courtesy of YNPRL.)

An avid hiker, guardian Galen Clark fearlessly explored all areas both in and outside Yosemite Valley and the Mariposa Grove. He is seen here at the Grizzly Giant. Just below Clark's feet on the card it reads, "Galen Clark, Discoverer of the Grove: Diameter 30 Feet, Circumference 104 Feet, Mark 1 1-2 Feet Thick." The bottom of the card reads, "Grizzly Giant, Mariposa Grove of Big Trees, California."

Galen Clark, besides serving two terms as guardian, was one of the best-known Yosemite figures. In later years, Clark was referred to as "Mr. Yosemite." Clark appears on many postcards, including this one at the Wawona Tree in the Mariposa Grove.

Sub-guardian or deputy ranger Stephen Cunningham worked mainly at the Mariposa Grove from 1878 into the 1880s. The Yosemite Park Commission directed that the guardian and sub-guardian were to always be on duty in Yosemite Valley and the Mariposa Grove during the visitor season. (Photograph by George Fiske; courtesy of YNPRL.)

Galen Clark is pictured here in front of the Haverford Tree in the Mariposa Grove. Clark built the cabin seen behind the tree for the convenience of visitors to the Grove. Clark was the best-known and most respected Yosemite state guardian.

"THE FALLEN MONARCH" AND 6TH U. S. CAVALRY, MARIPOSA GROVE, CAL.

In 1890, the Yosemite Forest Reserve was created around Yosemite Valley and the Mariposa Grove. This large reserve would eventually be named Yosemite National Park. In the early years, during the summer, U.S. Army cavalry troops patrolled the federal area, while the state area remained under civilian control of the guardian and Yosemite Park Commission. The cavalry administered and patrolled the federal park area until 1916.

In 1906, Yosemite Valley and the Mariposa Grove were returned to the federal government to become part of the larger Yosemite National Park. In 1916, the National Park Service (NPS) was formed and NPS rangers took over management of Yosemite. This postcard features NPS chief ranger Forest Townsley, who was a longtime and well-known Yosemite figure.

YOSEMITE NATIONAL PARK

342   CHIEF RANGER TOWNSLEY, WITH HIS PET CUB BEAR   118480

Entrance To California Redwood Park   Calif.

In 1903, the California Redwood Park at Big Basin was established. Note the lower part of the entrance sign that reads, "TO BE PRESERVED IN A STATE OF NATURE."

"ENTRANCE TO BASIN, CALIF."

The ranger station and residence is the building to the left of the California Redwood Park entrance sign. This was the south entrance to the park. Many parks still have rangers living in them to provide visitor services and protection on a 24-hour basis.

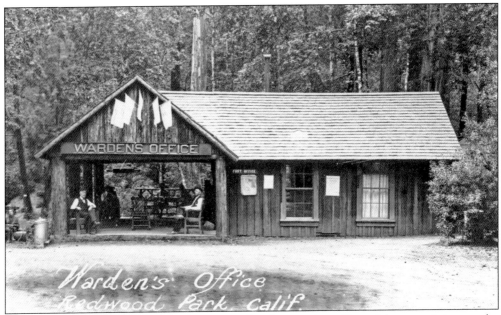

The Big Basin warden's office was the center of park operations. Two of the men sitting on the platform are thought to be an early warden and assistant warden. Most likely, it would have been William H. Dool, who served as warden from 1911 to 1931, and assistant warden Edward Park, who served from 1914 to 1934.

One of the popular visitor activities in the early days at the California Redwood Park was the "calling in" of the deer to be fed by rangers. Big Basin photographer Andrew P. Hill took this picture, probably in the 1920s. The front of the card reads, "Albert M. Weaver feeding the Wild Deer, California Redwood Park, Santa Cruz Co." (Photograph by Andrew P. Hill.)

This 1930s "big letter" postcard says, "Greetings from Big Basin Redwood State Park." The card features a small version of ranger Fred Canham "calling in the deer."

Taken sometime in the 1930s, this postcard featured warden Fred Moody and his patrol vehicle at the Big Basin Auto Tree. Redwood auto trees were very popular. The Big Basin tree was not a true drive-through tree, and vehicles had to be backed into the tree for pictures. Big Basin park photographer Roy Fulmer reported he took hundreds of pictures at the auto tree. (Photograph by F. Roy Fulmer.)

Ranger Leo Fry has his patrol car in the Big Basin Auto Tree sometime in 1940. Fry is also wearing the first ranger uniform, adopted the same year. The title park ranger was adopted five years later, replacing the park warden title used since 1905. (Photograph by F. Roy Fulmer.)

The log cabin design of the Armstrong Redwood Ranger Station is typical of park buildings in the 1930s or 1940s. Two unidentified rangers are standing next to the sign in front of the station.

The public's image of rangers as protectors of wildlife in parks is captured in this postcard. The card features a Los Angeles County park ranger in the 1930s. County park rangers often have responsibilities similar to those of state park rangers.

This postcard features the ranger station at Richardson Grove State Park on the Redwood Highway sometime after 1945. The sign over the door reads, "California State Park System" which is wording not in common use until the late 1940s.

In the 1930s, ranger William L. Kenyon peers at the Fallen Redwood Giant, one of the attractions at Richardson Grove State Park. This tree measures over 13 feet in diameter and stood over 300 feet tall. It is estimated that the tree was 1,250 years old when it fell. Protection of these magnificent trees from human and natural harm is one of the important responsibilities of rangers.

Roosevelt elk are fully protected by rangers at Prairie Creek Redwoods State Park. The ranger station is visible (with the flag poles) behind the elk area. Protection of the Roosevelt elk has been a ranger wildlife success story because at one time the elk had been reduced to just the single herd at Prairie Creek.

This is a personal "instant postcard" produced and sent out by ranger Dave Bartlett. Bartlett is on horse patrol here in August 1975 while working as part of a ranger exchange program with the National Park Service in Yosemite.

CALIFORNIA STATE PARK RANGERS

California State Park rangers celebrated their 125th anniversary in 1991. The back of this card reads, "California's State Park Rangers have been protecting state parks and serving the public since 1866. Today, 750 rangers and superintendents protect and manage nearly 300 state park units used by 73 million people a year." Pictured clockwise from top left are rangers Chuck Edgeman, Kevin Williams, and Joseph Mette. (Photographs by Frank S. Balthis.)

Ranger and author Jordan Fisher Smith distributed this postcard as a promotional item for his best-selling book *Nature Noir: A Park Ranger's Patrol in the Sierra*. The book is based on real life events during Smith's state ranger career. Mike Davis, author of *City of Quartz*, said, "I can't make up my mind whether Jordan Fisher Smith is John Muir at the crime scene or Elmore Leonard with a backpack."

Seven

RANGER SERVICE
PARK PROTECTION, PUBLIC SAFETY, AND PRESERVING THE PEACE

Protecting park resources was the first and most fundamental ranger responsibility, and it remains so to this day. This responsibility is the very basis of the ranger profession. The enforcement of park and general laws, preserving the peace, and "to arrest persons for the commission of public offenses" were also ranger responsibilities from the very beginning and continue to be so today.

In addition, from the beginning rangers have had to protect visitors from the parks' many hazards, including wild animals, poison oak, rushing water, and steep cliffs. Added to this is the requirement to respond to accidents, injuries, and lost persons.

This fundamental ranger work is often described as "protecting the park from people, protecting the people from the park, and protecting people from each other."

This work all started in May 1866 when ranger Galen Clark received an eight-page letter of instruction detailing his duties. Among other requirements, Clark was to strictly enforce the new state laws enacted to protect the park. By the 1890s, Yosemite rangers were officially authorized to "exercise general police supervision" and to "forbid and prevent all acts that tend to a breach of the peace, for the discomfiture of visitors, or injury or destruction to property."

Early rangers gave accounts of people problems. For instance, James Hutchings reported in 1882 that "sometimes we are visited by rough characters from the mountains, who, when crazy with liquor not only become nuisances but sometimes endanger human life." These same rough, crazed-with-liquor characters are unfortunately still visiting today's parks.

In 1928, modern legal peace officer and law enforcement authority was brought to rangers. Starting in 1970, rangers have received certified police training and have statewide general law enforcement authority. They are issued standard law police equipment, including firearms, pepper spray, batons, and handcuffs. Finally, they are provided higher levels of emergency medical training.

With higher levels of training, modern tools, and extensive authority, rangers have been able to preserve their positive image and provide the crucial public safety services needed for the 76 million people visiting state parks every year.

In 1870, Galen Clark made the first known park arrest of two men who cut down a large tree reportedly to improve the view from their room. Clark also wrote that "a small percentage of them [tourists] commit acts of malicious mischief and even serious damage." He went on to say that "mounted patrol men . . . would have a great restraining influence on this lawless class."

Ranger Anthony J. Trigeiro looks in disgust at the trash littering this campsite. He has his citation book out and is ready to give a ticket to anyone found responsible for this mess. In actuality, this is a picture taken at the state parks booth at the 1954 California State Fair. The exhibit's theme was the prevention of littering and the enforcement of littering laws. (Courtesy of CSP.)

At Pismo State Beach in 1964, two unidentified rangers bury a sea lion, reportedly shot to death. Protecting wildlife and other park resources—be it from poaching, vandalism, or inadvertent stupidity—is a top priority for rangers.

This airplane crash at Point Lobos in the 1960s brings a response by an unidentified ranger. Thousands of vehicle and visitor accidents occur every year in the park system. Rangers and state park lifeguards are normally the first responders to all of these incidents.

The notation with this picture said, "Getting ready to go on night patrol." In the photograph is ranger Al Whittington at Big Sur State Park in 1947 with his 1940 Ford patrol car. On the car is a "Division of Parks" decal, which was the first-ever state park door decal. By 1948, rangers were required by law to identify their regular patrol vehicles with door decals.

Ranger Jack P. Welch, stationed at Anza-Borrego Desert State Park, is on the radio in this 1959 picture. Due to its remoteness and large size, Anza-Borrego rangers were the first to get two-way radios in the 1950s. This very basic system, with no real dispatch center to contact, continued until the 1980s. Under the old system, when rangers were called out after hours they often had no radio communication.

This is a 4x4 Dodge Power Wagon outfitted as a fire truck and an unidentified ranger. In the early days of the parks, fighting wildfires was a regular part of the ranger job. However, by the 1960s, active firefighting had been transferred to the California Department of Forestry.

Ranger Randy Hogue puts up a "No Fireworks" sign just before the Fourth of July holiday at Mount Tamalpais in 1990. Rangers continue to have a very active role in fire prevention, including enforcement of fire laws, illegal use of fireworks, and illegal camping. (Photograph self-portrait by Randy Hogue.)

An unidentified ranger tries to prevent a fistfight in the 1970s. Bigger crowds and more nontraditional use of parks mean more public safety work for rangers.

One response to increased crime was to create a police canine handler position at Big Sur State Park, which in 1969 was being overrun by radical youths intent on ignoring the law. Pictured from left to right are canine handler ranger Richard Edwards, park canine Sam, a subject being arrested, and ranger Ronald McCall. Behind the group is a "paddy wagon" van designed for transporting multiple arrestees. Currently, there are 15 state park canine handler positions statewide.

A ranger patrol boat responds to a vessel fire. Starting in the 1950s, many lakes and reservoirs were added to the park system. The result is that rangers now operate the largest non-federal navy in the country and the state's largest boating enforcement program.

This line up of ranger patrol boats at Folsom Lake State Recreation Area in the 1970s reveals just a portion of the state park navy and the extent of the aquatic and boating program. On the boats are, from left to right, Thomas Lindsey, Garth Tanner, Rob Kilbourne, Ronald Angiers, Kenneth Grey, Gary Walter, John Melvin, and Walt Saylors. (Courtesy of CSP.)

Just barely visible in this poor quality Polaroid picture is ranger Denzil Verardo standing along the road as part of the security for the papal visit to Monterey in 1987. Over 30 rangers were assigned to the Pope's security detail. Other special assignments outside of the parks include the medfly outbreak in San Jose, various demonstrations, earthquakes, and homeland security duties following 9/11. (Courtesy of Denzil Verardo.)

Rangers Michelle Gardner (left) and Mikal Sandoval close Will Rogers State Park during the 1992 Los Angeles riots. Three state parks within the city limits were closed for four days to comply with the city's state of emergency and curfew during the riots. (Courtesy of Susan Ross.)

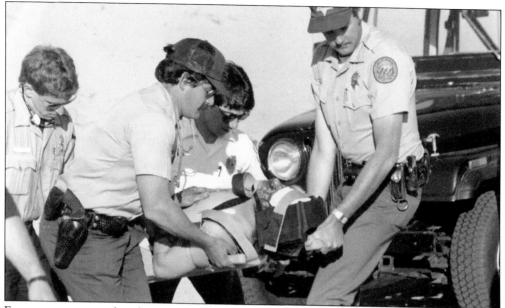

Emergency personnel and rangers move an accident victim at Oceano Dunes on Pismo State Beach. Pictured from left to right are an unidentified paramedic, ranger Jordan Fisher Smith, another unidentified medical responder, and ranger Alan Marshall. Oceano Dunes is one of six State Vehicular Recreation Areas (SVRAs) established for off-highway vehicle recreation operated by state parks. SVRAs have much higher accident and injury rates than other parks.

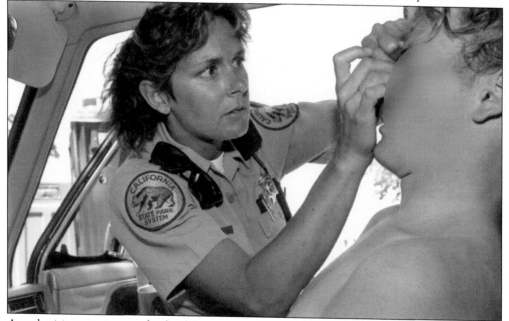

A park visitor receives medical aid from ranger L. Jill Dampier on July 5, 1990, at Folsom Lake State Recreation Area. The big summer three-day holiday weekends are not looked forward to by rangers. However, they mark the traditional beginning, middle, and end of the busy season. Dampier served as president of the California State Park Rangers Association in the 1990s. (Photograph by Janet Motenko.)

Ranger Jeff Price writes a nudity ticket on Black's Beach in San Diego County. Several unofficial nude beaches have developed in the park system. Although lewd behavior is never tolerated, the policy for simple nude sunbathing is more complicated. Although not officially condoned by department policy, nude sunbathing in remote areas is a low enforcement priority that normally requires the filing of a complaint before any action is taken.

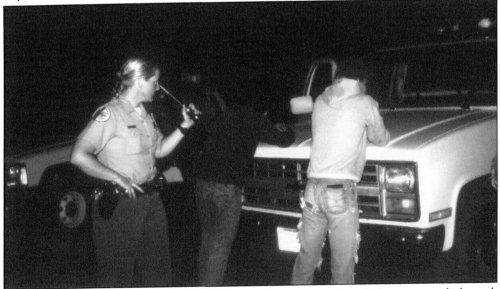

Ranger Tracy Becker stops two suspects at night at Pismo State Beach. Rangers regularly work night shifts and weekends. Traditionally, in most parks, rangers are only allowed one week of vacation between mid-May and mid-September. (Photograph by Brent MacGregor.)

Cartoonist Phil Frank captured some of the humorous aspects of the ranger job in his series of newspaper cartoons ultimately published in two books: *Asphalt State Park* and *Fur and Loafing in Yosemite*. For decades, Frank supported the two ranger associations in many ways, including drawing special cartoons for them. Frank was made an honorary state park ranger in 1990. (Courtesy of Phil Frank.)

Well, everything does not always go right when "ranging." No doubt ranger Donald Barnes got his patrol vehicle dug out and back in action very quickly.

The only ranger air patrol is at the 640,000-acre Anza-Borrego Desert State Park, the largest state park in the lower 48 states. Gene Hammock was the first ranger pilot in 1988, followed by Jon Muench in 1993. The third and current pilot, pictured here, is Kelly McCague who reports, "The plane is a Husky Aviat A-1. I like to call the park plane 'the Bear in the Air!'" (Photographs by Steve Bier; courtesy Kelly McCaque.)

Rafting ranger William Deitchman (left) pushes through the class IV Tunnel Chute rapids while on patrol on the Middle Fork of the American River in 2008. With Deitchman is park aid David Garcia. Deitchman has a one of a kind ranger job, administering a whitewater program that includes oversight of some 40 private rafting outfitters running commercial river trips on three different forks of the American River. (Courtesy of Hot Shot Imaging.)

Illegal marijuana gardens in state parks have been a constant problem since the 1970s. This 1983 image shows rangers James Burke (left) and Joseph Hardcastle working their way carefully through a marijuana garden. Hardcastle carries an 870 12-gauge shotgun, standard issue equipment normally carried in patrol vehicles.

Ranger Richard Bergstresser is carrying about 75 pounds of marijuana. Bergstresser related, "The raid was at Humboldt Redwoods in September 2006. The garden was about one mile in from the nearest road and about 800 feet up a very steep slope. It was maybe 60 plants with a weight of 200 pounds. It was one of 10 similar gardens destroyed in the park that year." (Courtesy of Richard Bergstresser.)

State parks is partners with an extensive number of federal, state, and local agencies, plus a wide variety of other groups. These numerous cooperative efforts include public safety responses, environmental issues, joint public use, and special events. Here meeting at a joint event at Candlestick Point State Park are, from left to right, an unidentified San Francisco police department (SFPD) lieutenant, Supt. Dan Dunge, another unidentified SFPD lieutenant, and ranger Noelle Holloway.

As out of the ordinary as it may seem, the bear that ranger Jenny Gardemeyer is checking out was legally shot outside of the park. Gardemeyer is verifying that the hunter has his correct licenses and tags. Bear hunting is not allowed in any state park, but some state park recreation areas allow deer, upland game, and/or duck hunting. (Photograph by Michael Lynch.)

Ranger Brian Robertson is doing a stolen weapons check on several firearms seized during a late night episode in a remote portion of the Auburn State Recreation Area. The incident was reported as "drunken illegal campers indiscriminately shooting up the neighborhood." Ranger Jeffrey Gaffney, in the background, watches over the two suspects sitting on the ground. (Photograph by Michael Lynch.)

This sequence of photographs documents ranger Donna Turner making a driving under the influence (DUI) contact and arrest in 2003. From left to right the pictures show Turner giving the DUI suspect a field breath test, searching him for weapons and/or contraband, and finally handcuffing the subject as the prelude to transporting and booking him into the Placer County Jail. (Photographs by Michael Lynch.)

Though hard to see, in the upper left portion of this picture is ranger Scott Struckman with his duty weapon pointed at a felony suspect. The suspect can be seen in the lower right portion of the picture with his hands up, partially sliding down a steep bank. The incident occurred on June 7, 2008, in the Auburn State Recreation Area. (Photograph by Philip Woods.)

Pictured is veteran ranger Sharon Gillian, who was shot and wounded on December 10, 2002, while citing an illegal camper at Henry Cowell Redwoods State Park. This was the first shooting of a state park ranger on record. The suspect was apprehended. State parks director Ruth Coleman said, "This is a startling reminder of the dangers faced by our rangers on a daily basis in patrolling the largest state park system in America." (Courtesy of CSP.)

Eight

RANGERS, CELEBRITIES, AND NOTABLES
RUBBING ELBOWS WITH THE STARS

Many park visitors want to get a picture with the ranger. This is pleasant for all concerned and good ranger public relations. However, rangers do not ordinarily solicit to have their picture taken. It is a different story though when a Hollywood celebrity, sports superstar, or well-known high government official shows up or is at a special event in the park.

For instance, ranger Chuck Bancroft related a story about a chance meeting with movie star Bill Murray at Point Lobos near Carmel: "One day I was in the kiosk giving a break to the park aid and this ratty old Land Cruiser comes driving in. Sure enough, there is Bill Murray with two buddies. He says to me, 'I'm thinking of buying this and wanted to test drive it around the area.' I said, in my best English accent, 'I am sorry, sir, this is Carmel, and we just couldn't let anything as disreputable as you or this car enter Point Lobos.' He laughed, and I laughed, and they entered the reserve. They were here for about an hour, and on the way out, I stopped them. I had grabbed a Stetson from the office and had the park aid take pictures of us."

The good news is that Bancroft got the picture with Murray, and it ran in the local newspaper. The bad news is that the original picture has been lost, so his picture is not in this book.

In another example, ranger Steve Johnson wrote, "The attached photo was taken during the filming of the David Mamet film *Things Change* in 1988. It was filmed at Sugar Pine Point State Park in Lake Tahoe and starred Don Ameche with Robert Prosky and Joe Mantegna. It was my opportunity to get to know David Mamet, Shel Silverstein (who was the cowriter), Robert Prosky, and Don Ameche. Along with the producer Michael Hausman, we all went shooting at a small firing range in Nevada. Great fun!"

Steve Johnson did not lose his Ameche picture, so it appears in this chapter.

The Forest Rangers, starring Fred MacMurray, Paulette Goddard, and Susan Hayward, was shot on location at Big Basin State Park in 1942. During the filming, star Susan Hayward fell off a log into 8 feet of water and had to be rescued. One can only hope that it was rangers who rescued the star, who reports said had "some bumps to the head and a bad scare."

The California State Park Rangers Association (CSPRA) made Walt Disney an honorary ranger in 1965 for producing a promotional film that was considered instrumental in the passage of the 1964 Park Bond Act. Making the presentation are, from left to right, CSPRA executive secretary Phil Geiger, CSPRA president Paul Griffin, and Walt Disney. Disney's daughter reported that Disney kept his honorary ranger plaque on the wall in his office and was quite proud of it.

Another honorary ranger is William "Bill" Lane, retired owner and publisher of *Sunset* magazine. The California State Park Rangers Association (CSPRA) honored Lane in 1997 for his lifetime contributions to the state parks. CSPRA president Gail Sevrens joins Lane in this picture taken at the 2008 Parks Conference. (Photograph by Janet Carle; courtesy of CSPRA.)

California governor Ronald Reagan (left), who would later become U.S. president Ronald Reagan, presents the California Medal of Valor to ranger William T. Parker in 1966. Parker earned the state's highest award by risking his life to rescue two women in heavy surf off the Sonoma Coast. The California Medal of Valor, awarded for "extraordinary acts of heroism," has been presented to over 20 park personnel since the award's inception in 1959.

California governor Edmund G. "Pat" Brown visits with rangers at Hearst Castle in 1961 during a ceremony marking the castle's millionth visitor. Chatting with the big boss are, from left to right, Ronald Rawlings, ? Hoover, John R. Flemming, and William R. Allison. Governor Brown was supportive of state parks during his two terms in office. (Courtesy of CSP.)

In 1984, ranger Bonnie Morse was awarded the California Medal of Valor by Gov. George Deukmejian. Morse received the award for her actions in saving three anglers whose boat capsized in strong wave action in the Salton Sea. Pictured at the presentation ceremony are, from left to right, state park director William Briner, Gov. George Deukmejian, Bonnie Morse, chief deputy director Garth Tanner, executive secretary Caryn Gordon, and Supt. Donald Hoyle.

Speaker of the state assembly Willie Brown (left), who would later become mayor of San Francisco, presents the California Medal of Valor to ranger Gary Strachan. Strachan was honored for risking his life in saving two swimmers caught in a riptide off Gold Bluffs Beach in 1980. In the background to the far right of the picture is Donna Pozzi, a longtime park employee, now chief of the interpretation and education division.

California governor Gray Davis poses with some of the state park staff in the Monterey District. Picture are, from left to right, district park and recreation specialist Dave Schaechtele, safety and enforcement specialist Dennis Hanson, district superintendent Lynn Rhodes, Gov. Gray Davis, park superintendent Phil Jenkins, park superintendent Stephanie Price, ranger Chuck Bancroft, and park maintenance worker Jason Byrd. (Courtesy of CSP.)

Ranger Robert Burke (left) lounges with the famous Sir Edmund Hillary who, in 1953, was the first person, along with Tenzing Norgay, to climb Mount Everest. Burke is visiting with Hillary, who was camping at Emerald Bay State Park at Lake Tahoe in 1999. (Courtesy of Robert Burke.)

Movie actor Clint Eastwood was filming the 1983 film *Sudden Impact* on location in the Monterey Bay area when this picture of him with ranger Lynn Rhodes was taken. The movie is probably best remembered for Dirty Harry's catch phrase, "Go ahead, make my day." Eastwood later went on to serve on the California State Park Commission. (Courtesy of Lynn Rhodes.)

The "Duke," John Wayne (left), plays chess at Hendy Woods State Park while supervising ranger Ed Tavares looks on. Wayne was filming a bank commercial in the park. He is playing chess with an unidentified friend. Tavares, a big John Wayne fan, reportedly got himself assigned as the state park monitor for the filming. (Courtesy of Sue and Ed Tavares.)

This picture of actor Don Ameche was taken during the filming of the David Mamet film *Things Change* in 1988 at Sugar Pine Point State Park at Lake Tahoe. From left to right are Don Ameche, ranger Steve Johnson, and Johnson's son. Johnson said, "It was my opportunity to get to know David Mamet, Robert Prosky, and Don. We all went shooting at a small firing range in Nevada. Great fun!" (Courtesy of Steve Johnson.)

Ranger David Carle (left) is pictured with Huell Howser, host of the popular television series *California's Gold*, during the filming of a segment at Mono Lake in July 1992. A fantastic promoter of state parks and cultural sites, Howser was made an honorary ranger by the California State Park Rangers Association in 2004. (Courtesy of David Carle.)

Shown here from left to right are district superintendent Lynn Rhodes; Huell Howser, the well-liked host of *California's Gold*; and Rick Hanks of the U.S. Bureau of Land Management. *California Gold* is one of the longest running and most beloved series about California ever produced. Howser has filmed hundreds of segments in state parks during the 17 years *California Gold* has been in production. (Courtesy of Lynn Rhodes.)

For nearly 60 years, John Lee Hooker (right) was one of the greatest bluesmen that performed. Hooker influenced countless generations of musicians and inspired music fans around the world, including ranger Tom Lindberg, seen here rocking out with the legend at China Camp State Park in the 1980s. (Courtesy of Tom Lindberg.)

The nationally known and universally revered Smokey Bear, for probably some good reason, is choking ranger Jay Galloway at Mount Tamalpais State Park. In reality, inside the Smokey outfit is Galloway's friend and ranger colleague Randy Hogue, and the two are just horsing around.

Stars and rangers line up during the 25th MASH reunion in 2008. MASH was originally filmed on what is now state park property. Pictured are, from left to right, director Charley Dubin, Mike "B. J. Hunnicut" Farrell, Loretta "Hot Lips" Swit, an unidentified producer, William "Fr. Francis Mulcahy" Christopher, another unidentified producer, Jeff "Igor the cook" Maxwell, district superintendent Ron Schafer, and park superintendent Al Pepito. (Courtesy of CSP.)

Dwayne "The Rock" Douglas (left) is a famous professional wrestler who has starred in several films, including *The Mummy Returns* and *The Scorpion King*. Luckily for ranger Danny Duarte, The Rock seems friendly enough, and Duarte apparently did not have to "go to the mat" with the star. (Courtesy of CSP.)

Cycling super star Lance Armstrong poses with a group of rangers at Russian Gulch State Park in the spring of 2006. Pictured are, from left to right, Patrick Freeling, Lance Armstrong, Mike Gleckler, Natalie Lohi, and Matt Khalar. (Courtesy of Patrick Freeling.)

Actor and fitness guru Richard Simmons has this group of rangers fired up and energized! Shot at Point Dume in Los Angeles County, the cheery group is, from left to right, ranger Dexter Crowder, Richard Simmons, ranger Darrell Readyhoff, and ranger Mark James. (Courtesy of CSP.)

Ranger Scott Liske (left) looks on while ranger and book author Michael Lynch jokingly handcuffs Mike Rowe, star of the *Dirty Jobs* series on the Discovery Channel. Rowe was filming a segment at the Auburn State Recreation Area on closing a dangerous abandoned mine shaft using super foam sealant.

Rangers are happy to pose with California first lady Maria Shriver, nationally known journalist and wife of Gov. Arnold Schwarzenegger. Pictured here from left to right are ranger Damon McJunkin, ranger Larry Fulmer, Maria Shriver, and ranger James Valdez. (Courtesy of CSP.)

Nine

THE PROFESSIONAL
GENERALIST
SINCE 1970

Starting in 1970 and continuing to this day is a period that could be called the era of the professional generalist ranger. In 1970, the ranger specifications were completely revised to remove all maintenance duties, require a college education, and seek candidates with a high degree of people skills. A yearlong training program was also introduced at this time that provided formal law enforcement, emergency medical, interpretive (outdoor education), and resource management training, all designed to produce a well-trained, well-rounded professional ranger.

The park system was undergoing massive changes and a massive expansion in the 1970s. The first modern full-time woman ranger, Paula Peterson, was hired in 1972. Many more women rangers were to follow. Also, major efforts were made to diversify the ranger workforce, to have it better reflect the make up of all the people in California. These diversified, college educated, highly trained, young professionals moved out into the parks by the hundreds in the 1970s, and some friction developed between them and the older "jack-of-all-trades" rangers.

The trend of more training and professionalism in all aspects of the ranger job has increased over time. Currently, initial law enforcement classroom and field training is eight months long. In addition, all rangers are now trained as Emergency Medical Responders (EMRs) or Emergency Medical Technicians (EMTs). Each ranger must also attend 24 hours of annual defensive tactics training and qualification a year. Finally, weapons training on 40-caliber semiautomatic pistols, 870 shotguns, and AR15 semiautomatic rifles is required quarterly.

On the park operation side, rangers must still patrol, train, perform public safety duties, provide information, and educate the public while they also administer many of the other visitor services. This includes overseeing a large number of seasonal employees and volunteers, who are the backbone of park operations. These seasonal employees and volunteers register campers, collect fees, issue permits, and perform a multitude of other jobs.

Carolyn Warner on the National Commission of Public Service put it this way, "Park Rangers: protectors, explainers, hosts, caretakers, people who are expected to be knowledgeable, helpful, courteous, and professional; people who find you when you're lost, help you when you're hurt, rescue you when you're stuck, and enforce the law when you or others can't abide by it."

In 1970, a formal professional training program replaced the previous on-the-job field training afforded to early rangers. A new training center was established at the Asilomar Conference Grounds in Pacific Grove. Visible to the camera are, from left to right, (first row) lifeguard Mike Tope, Dan Winkleman, Jean Ekstrom, Zackary Walker, Susan Ross, and Jeff Jones; (second row) Darlene ? and Ted Jackson; (third row) Charlie Edgemon and Ginger Henry of the training center staff.

Since the 1970s, all rangers have been required to complete the mandatory law enforcement training as established by the California Peace Officer Standards and Training (POST) Commission. This includes defensive tactics (DT) training and annual DT qualifications. Pictured in training are, from left to right, Mario Rodriguez, Steve Yamaichi, DT trainer Rod Stanford, Linda O'Kelley, and William "Bill" Berry. (Courtesy of CSP.)

The 1970s started a 30-year trend of increasing park use, like this crowd at Pismo State Beach. Overuse, crimes, accidents, and crowding all had negative impacts on the resources and the visitors' experience. Rangers had to directly confront these problems and work to minimize the impacts. The three-wheeled ATV motorcycle in the lower right corner of the picture is probably operating illegally in the protected sand dunes.

The sign at Big Basin State Park and ranger Wes King's body language tell it all: sorry, the park is full. Tens of thousands of visitors are turned away each year as campgrounds and picnic areas fill up, especially during the summer months and on weekends. Rangers and other park staff often take the brunt of a sometimes frustrated public when they cannot get into their favorite park.

Ranger Kathy Franklin is ready to go in her code 3 patrol vehicle at Morrow Bay State Park in 1986. Part of the positive ranger image is based on a friendly "works well with the public" manner, coupled with the training and proper equipment to deal with any and every kind of situation that arises in the parks.

A young visitor gets a telescopic look at geese on Folsom Lake with the aid of ranger Glen Walford. Even at high use and crowded recreation areas, the department works to provide more than just public safety services. In many parks, rangers or interpretive specialists only supervise the seasonal employees, and volunteers, who actually staff visitor centers, give campfire programs and lead guided hikes.

Rangers Scott Struckman and Jenny Gardemeyer provide emergency medical aid to an accident victim. Rangers are trained as Emergency Medical Responders (EMRs) or as Emergency Medical Technicians (EMTs) and respond to thousands of accidents and injuries statewide each year. (Photograph by Scott Liske.)

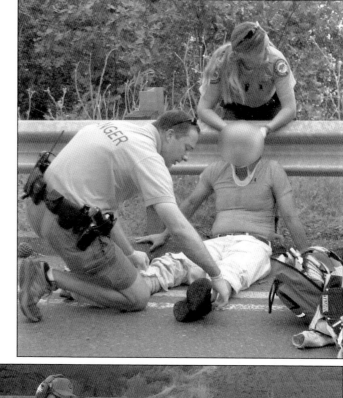

Firearms training and quarterly qualification are mandated for all rangers. Firearms instructor Scott Liske (center) checks out ranger Zack Hawkins as he reloads his AR15 semiautomatic rifle during firearms qualifications. Behind Liske, ranger Mark Hada points his 40-caliber pistol down range at a target. Police 870 shotguns are also part of the law enforcement equipment carried by rangers in their patrol vehicles. (Photograph by Michael Lynch.)

In the 1990s, ranger sports-type cards became popular as handouts and fancy business cards. Clockwise, the cards picture (top left, from left to right) rangers D. Michael Van Hook, John Cleary, Greg Wells, Jordan Fisher Smith, and Michael Lynch; (top right) ranger Mike Smittle and his canine partner, Bessy; (bottom right) ranger Alexandra Ott Robertson; and (bottom left) ranger John Russo and his German shepherd partner, Watz.

The State Park Peace Officers Association of California (SPPOAC) was organized in 1979 to represent rangers on labor issues. The 1990 SPPOAC Board of Directors are, from left to right (first row) state parks director Henry Agonia, Nancy Fuller, Vic Trevisanut, deputy director Lee Chauvet, Bob Burke, and chief deputy director Jack Harrison, (second row) Lisa Mulz, Susan Grove, Joe Von Hermann, Ken Morse, Mike French, Juvie Ortiz III, Steve Johnson, and Vern McHenry.

Nineteen ninety-one marked the 125th anniversary of state park rangers. The governor, legislature, and various other organizations officially recognized this milestone as the "Year of the Ranger." A 125th Ranger Anniversary Committee organized a year of events, displays, publications, and even a video. Meeting in Yosemite, 125th committee members are, from left to right, Kirk Wallace, Susan Ross, Michael Lynch, Nedva Martinez, Paula Peterson, Jackie Ball, Bill Monaghan, and Donald Murphy.

The International Ranger Federation (IRF) bonds together park rangers from around the world. Shown here at the World Ranger Conference in Costa Rica in 1997 are, from left to right, national park service ranger Jeff Ohlfs, an unidentified Spanish park ranger, California state park ranger Michael Whitehead, and an unidentified park ranger from Argentina. The California State Park Rangers Association is a member of the IRF.

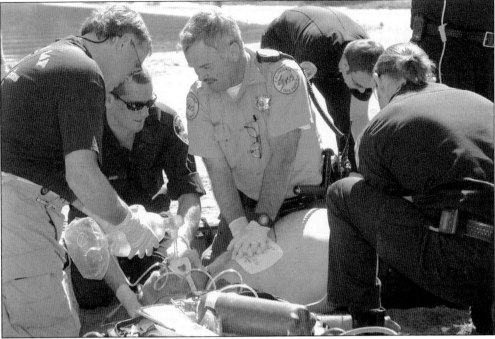

A clam digger collapsed at Sonoma Coast State Beach on March 31, 2005, from a massive heart attack. Ranger Rich Lawton was first on scene, followed by other county emergency responders. Performing CPR on the victim are, from left to right, an unidentified emergency medial responder, seasonal lifeguard Nate Buck, Rich Lawton, and two more unidentified responders. Sadly, the victim did not survive. (Courtesy of the *Bodega Bay Navigator*; photograph by Joel Hack.)

Ranger Bob Burke poses with a group of young visitors or possibly junior rangers at Lake Tahoe. Rangers, depending on their assignment, have and will continue to provide public information and educational and interpretive programs to visitors and groups. Rangers have to be flexible though. At a moment's notice they may have to go from kids to crime.

A suspect is arrested and cuffed by ranger Scott Liske in a multi-agency raid on marijuana grown on state park property in 2007. Rangers regularly participate in these types of multiagency operations, including marijuana raids on public lands, joint boating enforcement operations, and DUI checkpoints.

Ranger Kevin Williams surveys the elephant seal population at Ano Nuevo State Reserve. Protecting and preserving California's natural and cultural resources, educating the public about these treasures, and providing safe and enjoyable access to the state parks have always been and will continue to be a primary duty of state park rangers. (Photograph by Frank Balthis.)

Ranger Brian Robertson blocks off the road as a Cal Star air ambulance lands to pick up an accident victim in the Auburn State Recreation Area. An unidentified Cal Fire firefighter in the background blocks the other side. Public safety duties, including law enforcement, resource protection, rescue, and emergency medical aid are essential core responsibilities of rangers now and into the future. (Photograph by Jenny Gardemeyer.)

The State Park Peace Officers Association of California (SPPOAC) launched a campaign in recent years to educate the legislature and public on the issues regarding the chronic shortages in the ranger ranks. SPPOAC points out that this situation is in large part due to the great disparity in the pay and benefits of rangers when compared to other peace officers. Ranger Robert Burke is featured on this SPPOAC publication.

Unlike in earlier years, state parks have suffered an ongoing shortage of rangers and lifeguards and some difficulty in attracting sufficient new applicants. Factors for this may include relatively low pay, rigorous background checks, and an extensive nine-month training program. One message this recruitment poster might inadvertently suggest is that rangers and lifeguards "get paid in sunsets." Pictured are lifeguard Eddie Rhee-Pizano and ranger Elizabeth Moore. (Courtesy of CSP.)

Rangers are part of a team of park employees dedicated to the parks and the public. State parks director Ruth Coleman put it this way: "All those who work with tireless dedication to preserve and protect our resources and enhance the experience of our visitors must be complimented." From left to right are ranger Rodger Hood, equipment operator Marc Johnston, maintenance worker Mark Kimberlin, and senior park aid Richard Nevarez at the Auburn State Recreation Area.

The top state park ranger brass are, from left to right, law enforcement and emergency services chief Lynn Rhodes, deputy director for operations Theodore "Ted" Jackson, and off-highway motor vehicle recreation division chief Phil Jenkins. Not pictured is southern field division chief Tony Perez. As state parks' top cop, Jackson oversees the law enforcement efforts of more than 500 peace officers, the second largest law enforcement group in state service.

State parks director Ruth Coleman (left) talks to park superintendent Mark Gibson (center) and district superintendent Scott Nakaji at a museum dedication at Marshall Gold Discovery State Historic Park in 2007. Director Coleman said, "We have a ranger force that is especially dedicated to our mission" and added, "It is a team effort and all those who work with tireless dedication to preserve and protect our resources . . . must be recognized." (Photograph by Redi Lee.)

Gov. Arnold Schwarzenegger proclaimed July 31, 2007, "California State Park Ranger Day" and said, "California is blessed to be the home of a fantastic state park system, containing more than 270 natural places and cultural heritage sites. Thanks to our dedicated state park rangers and support personnel, our parks' beauty and safety are enjoyed every year by 76 million visitors . . . By overseeing 1.5 million acres of mountains, beaches, deserts, and nearly every other kind of terrain imaginable, our 400 state park rangers have a tremendous responsibility. They develop conservation programs, monitor environmental health, and respond to emergencies. As fully sworn peace officers, state park rangers keep California safe, while providing a vital link between our parks and the public. Their service to our state is truly remarkable, and their stewardship of our natural resources honors our proud environmental heritage. I encourage all Californians to join me in paying tribute to the men and women who preserve our state's natural and cultural treasures." From left to right are park superintendent Stephanie Price, Gov. Arnold Schwarzenegger, and park superintendent Curtis L. Price. (Courtesy of the California Governor's Office.)

DISCOVER THOUSANDS OF LOCAL HISTORY BOOKS FEATURING MILLIONS OF VINTAGE IMAGES

Arcadia Publishing, the leading local history publisher in the United States, is committed to making history accessible and meaningful through publishing books that celebrate and preserve the heritage of America's people and places.

Find more books like this at
www.arcadiapublishing.com

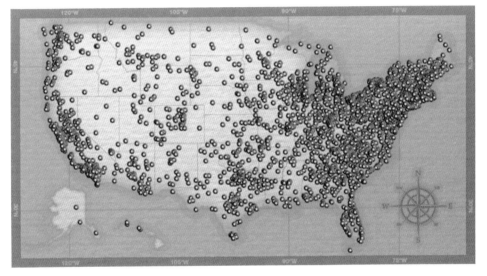

Search for your hometown history, your old stomping grounds, and even your favorite sports team.

Consistent with our mission to preserve history on a local level, this book was printed in South Carolina on American-made paper and manufactured entirely in the United States. Products carrying the accredited Forest Stewardship Council (FSC) label are printed on 100 percent FSC-certified paper.